HERALDICA COLLEGII CARDINALIUM

A Roll of Arms of the College of Cardinals
Supplement I
2002

Michael Francis McCarthy

Thylacine Press
2002

First Published 2002 by

THYLACINE PRESS
8 Little Surrey Street
DARLINGHURST NSW 2011
email: thylacinepress@bigpond.com
Website:
ABN: 91 641 984 498

Previous works:

An Armorial of the Hierarchy of the Catholic Church in Australia 1998
Heraldica Collegii Cardinalium 1800 to 2000 2000
Armoria Sedium 2001
Heraldica Collegii Cardinalium 1198 to 1799 2002

National Library of Australia
in-publishing entry:

McCarthy, Michael Francis
Heraldica Collegii Cardinalium

Bibliography
Index

ISBN 0-9577947-2-X

Printed by the University Printing Service
University of Sydney

SUPPLEMENT I

For the Consistory of 21 February 2001

This is the first planned supplement to my *Heraldica Collegii Cardinalium* and will be followed by others as new Cardinals are created. It includes the two Cardinals *created in petto* in 1998 and all those created in 2001.

It also includes any amendments to the above which have come to light since its publication. These will be found from page 27 on.

I would also like to include here a formal apology to my mentor and friend Archbishop Bruno Heim for my unforgivable error in spelling his name incorrectly in the dedication of the above. Dyslexia is regrettably one of my lesser known talents.

I would also like to extend my gratitude to *Don Raffaele Farina SDB*, Prefect of the Vatican Library and *Dr. Luigina Orlandi* of the Vatican Library for their assistance in gathering the various arms of the Cardinals created in 2001

Consistories in this supplement held by John Paul II

21st February 1998
(and held in Petto - Proclaimed 21st February 2001)

JAWORSKI
PUJATS

21ST February 2001

RE
NGUYEN VAN THUAN
CACCIAVILLAN
SEBASTIANI
GROCHOLEWSKI
SARAIVA MARTINS
DAOUD
POMPEDDA
KASPER
DEGENHARDT
GONZALES ZUMARRAGA
DIAS
AGNELO
RUBIANO SAENZ
McCARRICK
CONNELL
BACKIS
ERRAZURIS OSSA
TERRAZAS SANDOVAL
NAPIER
RODRIGUEZ MARADIAGA
AGRE
BILLE
VELASCO GARVIA
CIPRIANI THORNE
ALVAREZ MARTINEZ
HUMMES
VITHAYATHIL
BERGOGLIO
POLICARPO
POLETTO
MURPHY-O'CONNOR
EGAN
HUSAR
LEHMAN
GHATTAS
HONORE
TUCCI
SCHEFFCZYK
DULLES

Geraldo Majella AGNELO
S. Gregorio Magna alla Magliana
21-II-2001
Archbishop of Sao Salvador da Bahia
Primate of Brasil
1933-

ARMS,- Argent, on a cross cape in base azure between four hearts enflamed en pairle gules, a mullet argent.

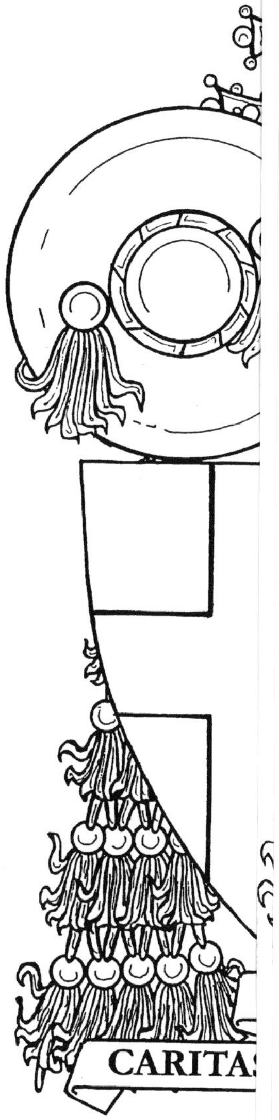

Pedro RUBIAN
Trasfigurazione
21-II-20
Archbishop of
Primate of Co
1932-

ARMS,- Gules, a cross or.

Agostin
Ss. Angeli C

Archbi

ARMS,- Azure, fro and azure, three c (6) argent.

Heraldica Collegii Cardinalium Supplement I

Marian JAWORSKI
S. Sisto
In petto 21-II-1998
Proclaimed 21-II-2001
Archbishop of Lviv of the Latins
Ukraine
1926-

ARMS,- Gules, a bishop on full pontificals genuflecting or.

Janis PUJATS
S. Silvia
In petto 21-II-1998
Proclaimed 21-II-2001
Archbishop of Riga
Latvia
1930-

ARMS,- Azure, on a bend argent between in chief o a champagne or on water issuant barry wavy argent and azure, three churches argent; and in base on a base or a church with two spires argent, a road wavy in pale argent; issuant from the base a latin cross or and in base issuant a rose slipped or; the Words TERRA MARIANA sable.

Antonio Jose GONZALES ZUMARRAGA
S. Maria in Via
21-II-2001
Archbishop of Quito
Primate of Ecuador
1925-

ARMS,- Gules, the monogram "XP" or, on a chief azure a star(6) argent.

Theodore Edgar McCARRICK
Ss. Nereo ed Achilleo
21-II-2001
Archbishop of Washington
USA
1930-

ARMS,- WASHINGTON impaling gules, on a cross roundant or between in 1st a rock argent; in 2nd a lion rampant or; in 3rd a sun issuant from the canton or and in 4th three ermine spots argent, a coronet azure.

Desmond CONNELL
S. Silvestro in Capite
21-II-2001
Archbishop of Dublin
Primate of Ireland
1926-

ARMS,- DUBLIN impaling per fess argent and vert, a stag trippant proper between at dexter chief an ear of wheat slipped or, at sinister chief a bunch of grapes proper and in base a lily slipped argent.

Agostino CACCIAVILLAN
Ss. Angeli Custodi a Citta Giardino
21-II-2001
Archbishop of Amiterno
Italy
1926-

ARMS,- Azure, from a base barry wavy argent and azure, three colle issuant or below a star (6) argent.

Sergio SEBASTIANI
S. Eustachio
21-II-2001
Archbishop of Cesarea di Mauritania
Italy
1931-

ARMS,- Azure, three annulets interlaced argent, a chief gules, three fleur-de-lis argent.

Zenon GROCHOLEWSKI
S. Nicolo in Carcere
21-II-2001
Archbishop of Agropoli
Poland
1939-

ARMS,- Gules, cape ploye azure, in dexter chief an eagle displayed argent, membered or; in sinister chief two keys in saltire, that in bend or, that in bend sinister argent, corded or; and in base the monogram "XP" or below a star (6) argent.

Jose SARAIVA MARTINS Cmf
Nostra Signora del S. Cuore
21-II-2001
Archbishop of Tuburnica
Italy
1932

ARMS,- Per fess and in chief per pale; 1. Azure, the monogram "XP" or; 2. Azure, a globe argent, marked sable ensigned with a cross or; 3. Gules, six colle issuant ensigned with a smaller seventh argent between at dexter a star (6) or.

Crescenzio SEPE
Dio Padre Misericordioso
21-II-2001
Archbishop of Grado
Italy
1943-
ARMS,- Azure, the monogram "XP" issuant from an anchor between at dexter the letter "A" and at sinister "W" and below a star (8) or.

Jorge Maria MEIJA
S. Girolamo della Carita
21-II-2001
Archbishop of Apollonia
Argentina
1923-
ARMS,- Gules, three pallets ermine impaling azure a lion rampant or.

Ignace Moussa I DAOUD
Cardinal Patriarch
21-II-2001
Patriarch Emeritus of Antioch of the Syrians
Syria
1930-
ARMS,- Gules, an open book in fess argent, bound or debruised in base by a chalice or and all below a dove soarant proper, nimed.

Mario Francesco POMPEDDA
L'Annunciazione della B.V.M a Via Ardeatina
21-II-2001
Archbishop of Bisarcio
Italy
1929-
ARMS,- Per fess azure, a mountain issuant or below in sinister canton a star (8) argent AND gules, a set of scales argent.

Walter KASPER
Ognissanti in Via Apia Nuova
21-II-2001
Bishop Emeritus of Rottenburg-Stuttgart
Germany
1933-

ARMS,- Quarterly; 1&4. Sable a cross or ROTTENBURG-STUTTGART; 2. Azure, a house argent, roofed or and 3. Azure, a bunch of grapes argent on the vine or.

Johannes Joachim DEGENHARTDT
S. Liborio
21-II-2001
Archbishop of Paderborn
Germany
1926-2002

ARMS,- Quarterly; 1. Gules a cross or PADERBORN; 2. Or, on an open book argent bound gules; the letters "A" and "Ω" sable; 3. Azure, three besants jessant de lis or, one and two; 4. Argent, a cross moline gules PYRMONT.

Antonio Jose GONZALES ZUMARRAGA
S. Maria in Via
21-II-2001
Archbishop of Quito
Primate of Ecuador
1925-
ARMS,- Gules, the monogram "XP" or, on a chief azure a star(6) argent.

Ivan DIAS
Spirito Santo alla Ferratella
21-II-2001
Archbishop of Bombay
India
1936-
ARMS,- Azure, a fleur-de-lis or, on a chief gules a ducal coronet or.

Geraldo Majella AGNELO
S. Gregorio Magna alla Magliana
21-II-2001
Archbishop of Sao Salvador da Bahia
Primate of Brasil
1933-

ARMS,- Argent, on a cross cape in base azure between four hearts enflamed en pairle gules, a mullet argent.

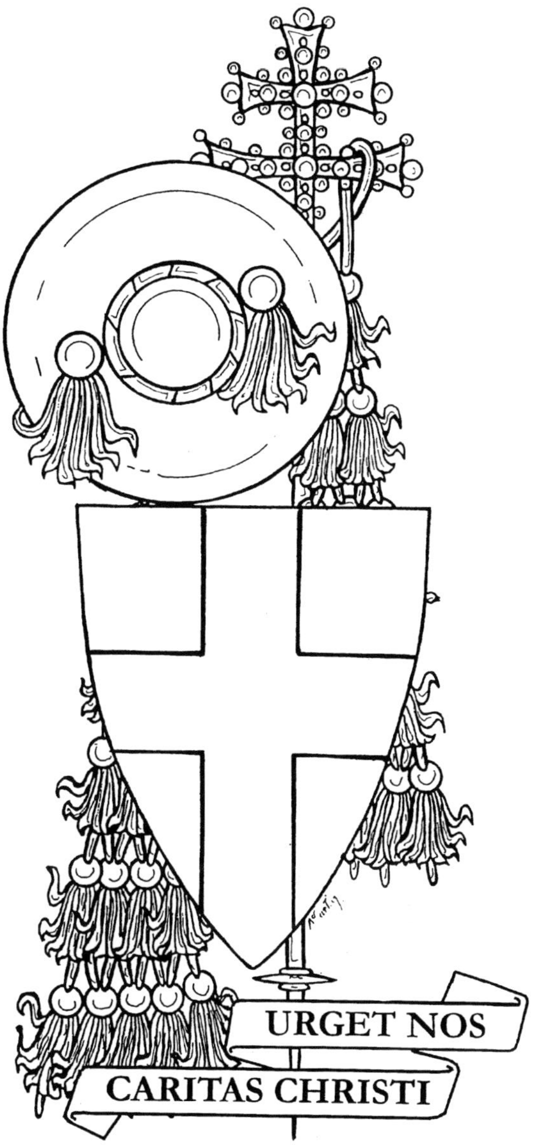

Pedro RUBIANO SAENZ
Trasfigurazione di N.S.G.C.
21-II-2001
Archbishop of Bogota
Primate of Colombia
1932-

ARMS,- Gules, a cross or.

Theodore Edgar McCARRICK
Ss. Nereo ed Achilleo
21-II-2001
Archbishop of Washington
USA
1930-

ARMS,- WASHINGTON impaling gules, on a cross roundant or between in 1st a rock argent; in 2nd a lion rampant or; in 3rd a sun issuant from the canton or and in 4th three ermine spots argent, a coronet azure.

Desmond CONNELL
S. Silvestro in Capite
21-II-2001
Archbishop of Dublin
Primate of Ireland
1926-

ARMS,- DUBLIN impaling per fess argent and vert, a stag trippant proper between at dexter chief an ear of wheat slipped or, at sinister chief a bunch of grapes proper and in base a lily slipped argent.

Audrys Juozas BACKIS
Nativita di N.S.G.C.
21-II-2001
Archbishop of Vilnius
Lithuania
1937-

ARMS,- Azure, a fleur-de-lis argent on a chief nebully or three cartouches per pale azure and gules, a patriarchial cross couped argent.

Francisco Javier ERRAZURIS OSSA
S. Maria della Pace
21-II-2001
Archbishop of Santiago de Chile
Primate of Chile
1933-

ARMS,- Or, the BVM proper a border azure, seme of escallops or.

Julio TERRAZAS SANDOVAL Cssr
S. Giovanni Battista de'Rossi
21-II-2001
Archbishop of Santa Cruz de la Sierra
Bolivia
1936-

ARMS,-Azure, a base vert, four colle issuant over the base or; in chief a mullets or between at dexter three ears of wheat cojoined issuant from the base and at sinister a latin cross couped gules.

Wilfrid Fox NAPIER
S. Francesco d'Assisi ad Acilae
21-II-2001
Archbishop of Durban
South Africa
1941-

ARMS,- Tierce in pairle reversed; 1. Azure, an escutcheon gules, a modern pallium issuant proper between in chief a mullet argent;.2. Or, on an escutcheon argent, a saltire between four roses gules charged with five escallops argent; 3. The Franciscan Order; Surtout, gules, a dove descendant argent, nimed or.

Oscar Andres
RODRIGUEZ MARADIAGA Sdb
S. Maria della Speranza
21-II-2001
Archbishop of Tegucigalpa
Honduras
1942-

ARMS,- Azure, on a cross or debruising a net in arc argent and between in the 2nd a star (8) or, a boat in fess azure debruised by a sword in pale proper.

Bernard AGRE
S. Giovanni Crisostomo a Monte Sacro Alto
21-II-2001
Archbishop of Adidjan
Ivory Coast
1926-

ARMS,- Vert, a fissure in dexter barry wavy argent and azure, this plugged in chief by a rock sable, extending on to a chief gules and ensigned with a cross or and in sinister a mullet reversed or

Louis-Marie BILLE
Ss. Trinita al Monte Pincio
21-II-2001
Archbishop of Lyons
Primate of Gaul
France
1938-2002
ARMS,- Did not use arms.

Ignacio Antonio VELASCO GARCIA Sdb
S. Maria Domenica Mazzarello
21-II-2001
Archbishop of Caracas
Primate of Venezuela
1929-
ARMS,- Per fess; 1. Per fess azure and sable, the initial "M" ensigned with a coronet or; 2. Gules, seme of tongues of flame or.

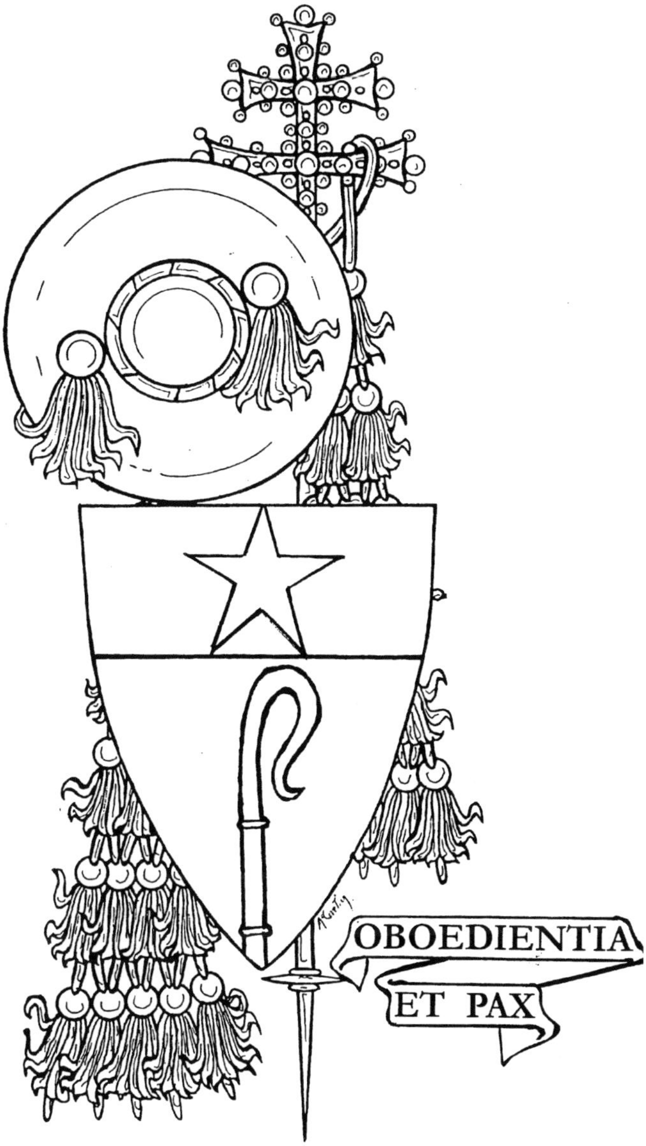

Juan Luis CIPRIANI THORNE Opus Dei
S. Camillo de Lellis
21-II-2001
Archbishop of Lima
Primate of Peru
1943-
ARMS,- Per bend gules and vert, on a bend argent between in chief a star (8) and in base a tower or, three eagles displayed in bend sable crowned and membered or.

Francisco ALVAREZ MARTINEZ
S. Maria "Regina Pacis" a Monte Verde
21-II-2001
Archbishop of Toledo
Primate of Spain
1925-
ARMS,- Vert, a crozier issuant or, on a chief azure a mullet argent.

Claudio HUMMES Ofm
S. Antonio da Padova in Via Merulana
21-II-2001
Archbishop of Sao Paulo
Brasil
1934-

ARMS,- Per pale or, a sword deflected in bend sinister or debruised by an open book argent, bound or, overall in bend a palm frond or; impaling argent, the badge of the Franciscans proper; Overall a chief azure, a sun in splendor or.

Varkey VITHAYATHIL Cssr
S. Bernardo alle Terme
21-II-2001
Archbishop Major of Ernakulum-Angamaly
India
1927-

ARMS,- Azure, a globe vert charged with an image of St. Thomas proper and debruised in base by an open book argent, bound or charged with an Indian lamp enflamed proper; all below at dexter chief a representation of the annunciation and in sinister chief four arms, vested, clasped in friendship argent.

Jorge Mario BERGOGLIO Sj
S. Roberto Bellarmino
21-II-2001
Archbishop of Buenos Aires
Primate of Argentina
1936-
ARMS,- Azure, the Jesuit sun proper above a mullet or and a marigold slipped proper.

Jose da CRUZ POLICARPO
S. Antonio in Campo Marzio
21-II-2001
Patriarch of Lisbon
Primate of Portugal
1936-
ARMS,- Vert, on a cross argent, a pomegranate plant vert slipped proper with nine pods.

Severino POLETTO
S. Giuseppe in Via Trionfale
21-II-2001
Archbishop of Turin
Italy
1933-
ARMS,- Gules, on a mount issuant vert, a cross or with therefrom a road wavy argent, in sinister an olive branch issuant proper; a chief argent, cape reversed azure a star (8) or.

Cormac MURPHY-O'CONNOR
S. Maria sopra Minerva
21-II-2001
Archbishop of Westminster
Primus inter Pares in England and Wales
United Kingdom
1932-
ARMS,- WESTMINSTER impaling azure, an oak tree fructed and eradicated supported in sinister by a lion rampant or, in chief three fleur-de-lis or.

Edward Michael EGAN
Ss. Giovanni e Paolo
21-II-2001
Archbishop of New York
USA
1932-

ARMS,- NEW YORK impaling azure, a Celtic cross couped or charged with four olive branches in cross vert and there over a dove in flight in bend proper

Lubomyr HUSAR
S. Sofia a Via Boccea
21-II-2001
Archbishop Major of Lviv of the Ukrainians
Primate of Galitz
Ukraine
1933-

ARMS,- Or, a representation of an Icon of the BVM and child proper, a bend canton azure, from an island vert a cross enfiled of a crown of thorns and a spear and tipped read in saltire all or.

Karl LEHMANN
S. Leone I
21-II-2001
Bishop of Mainz
Germany
1936-

ARMS,- MAINZ quartering WORMS; surtout or, an open book gules with thereon "A" and "Ω" or.

Stephanos II GHATTAS CM
Cardinal Patriarch
21-II-2001
Patriarch of Alessandria of the Copts
Egypt
1920-

ARMS,- Azure, a saltire or between in chief a star (8) argent; in dexter fess a torch enflamed between a wreath all or; in sinister three pyramids argent above a lily slipped proper; and in base an Egyptian scene proper.

Jean HONORE
S. Maria della Salute a Primavalle
21-II-2001
Archbishop Emeritus of Tours
France
1920-
ARMS,- Does not use arms.

Roberto TUCCI Sj
S. Ignazio di Loyola a Campo Marzio
21-II-2001
Italy
1921-
ARMS,- Azure, cape argent, in chief overall a dove soarant proper and on the cape in base two arms vested issuant and clasped argent, the sinister charged with a cross couped gules.

Leo SCHEFFCZYK
S. Francesco Saverio alla Garbatella
21-II-2001
Italy
1920-

ARMS,- Azure, a pale of three pallets and a fess of three barrulets interlaced or; overall a heart pierced guttee gules ensigned with a crossed crown of thorns or; a border or, seme of tongues of flame gules.

Avery DULLES Sj
Ss. Nomi di Gesu e Maria in Via Lata
21-II-2001
USA
1918-

ARMS,- Per fess Or a plate charged with "IHS" sable between at dexter three nails en pairle gules and at sinister a star(8) gules above two wavy bars sable; And azure, three fleur-de-lis or.

AMENDMENTS TO VOLUME II (1800-2000)

1.

2.

3.

4.

Advice has been received of the following amendments and is included here to correct the detected errors.

1. *Fabrizio SCEBARRAS TESTAFERRATA (PAGE 42) -Arms should be - Gules, a Roman soldier's armour and helm or impaling argent, a bull forcenee gules, a chief azure, three stars (8) or.*
2. *Antonio MATTEUCCI (page 152) - Arms should be - Azure, a falcon statant on six colle issuant holding in its talon a lion's head all or.*
3. *Klemens August von GALEN (page 357)- Arms should be- Or, a fess gules MUNSTER impaling Quarterly 1&4 Argent three wolf hooks gules; 2&3 Argent a key in pale or. (sometime Munster, surtout the personal quartered arms).*
4. *Gilberto AGUSTONI (page 537) - Arms should be Per pale Gules and azure, a cross pommetty fitchee or at dexter debruised by a lamb springant throughout argent which is debruised in sinister with a tower argent.*
5. *Dario CASTRILLON HOYOS (page 547) - Arms should be - Vert a Latin cross couped or impaling azure, a double tower argent below in chief a mullet fesswise or and in base three mountains argent rising from a plain vert, a stream proper.*
6. *Giovanni CHELI (page 554) has changed his arms to - Per fess argent, a star (8) sable, and sable two stars (8) argent.*
7. *Donato Maria dell'OLIO (PAGE 246)- Motto is "PRAEMIUM ISTITIAE PAX".*
8. *James Cardinal McINTYRE's full name was James Francis Aloysius McIntrye. Previously his third name was given as Louis. (page 366).*
9. *Aurelio SABATTIANI (page 485) - Motto should be "RADICATUS IN CARITATIS".*

5.

6.

INDEX

STOP PRESS

The following were received on 15th November 2002:

Dino MONDUZZI (page 555)

Arms, - JOHN PAUL II impaling gules, three roses in chevron or above three mounts issuant argent; on a chief argent a comet or.

ISBN 9780957794726